10X YOUR SALES EFFECTIVENESS NOW

By Tightening Loose Connections

Chander Shekhar Sibal

Worldwide Published by
Pendown Press

PENDOWN PRESS
An ISO 9001 & ISO 14001 Certified Co.,
Regd. Office: 2525/193, 1st Floor, Onkar Nagar-A,
Tri Nagar, Delhi-110035
Ph.: 09350849407, 09312235086
E-mail: info@pendownpress.com
Branch Office: 1A/2A, 20, Hari Sadan, Ansari Road,
Daryaganj, New Delhi-110002
Ph.: 011-45794768
Website: PendownPress.com

First Edition: 2020
Price: ₹259/-
ISBN: 978-93-89601-69-5

Layout and Cover Designed by Pendown Graphics Team
Printed and Bound in India by Thomson Press India Ltd.

10X YOUR SALES EFFECTIVENESS NOW

By Tightening Loose Connections

CONTENTS

Preface i

Acknowledgements iii

Why This Book vii

01

What is Sales? 1

02

Loose Connections 5

03

Dig Deeper 7

04

Convince; Convince and Convince 11

05

Never Say Die 13

06

Never Lose your Heart 15

07

Be Positive 17

08
Integrity is the Best Policy 19

09
Tough Competition ? Innovate 21

10
Be Early and consultative selling can be of big Help 23

11
Learn to Listen 27

12
Humor sells! 29

13
Think Big, Think Long Term 31

14
Making Organisation Structure that fosters Teamwork & Entrepreneurial skills 35

15
Winning Cycle 39

The purpose of the book is to give back to society by empowering youngsters with self- confidence to realize their true potential.

PREFACE

Over the last three decades of my experience in the Indian Healthcare Industry, I have had the privilege of seeing the sector grow from scratch to noticeable heights. I started my journey as a Service Engineer, Customer Engineer and then keep on adding Sales, Product Management, Marketing and P&L roles.

With this book, I have made an attempt to share my experiences and insights–the first and foremost of which is that there is no magic.

Instead, passion, hard work, integrity, team work, dedication and simplicity, are key to overcoming barriers and achieving targets consistently. Presence of mind, a cool head and common sense are often more than enough to solve the knottiest of problems. In our rush to build new connections, we should not forget to maintain relationships and provide service, whenever required.

The Gita exhorts us to do our duties with single-minded attention without thinking of the results. And I believe this is the best way to achieve anything in life–even in Sales. We should do our karma and leave everything else to God. The rest will follow–you just have to have faith.

ACKNOWLEDGEMENTS

I would like to thank my wife Dr. Priti Nanda Sibal who took me for the workshop done by Mr. Akshar Yadav on "How to write your own book" and the result is here for everyone to see. I would also like to thank my parents Sh. B.L. Sibal ji and Smt. Sudesh Sibal ji for guiding and instilling hard work, dedication, discipline and honesty which helped shape not only my character, but also career. I would like to thank my Father and Mother inlaw Mr. MK Nanda and Mrs. Shashibala Nanda for their love , affection and guidance in life.

I would like to thank Mr. Dinesh Verma for the motivation to write this book. I would also like to acknowledge my Sons Apurv Sibal and Averal Sibal with whom I try to reach some middle ground and understand how the younger generation think. Thanks to all my colleagues, especially Mr. Sunil Khurana, Mr. J. S. Sirari, Mr. Kenichi Tanaka, Mr. Haan, Mr. Anurag Gupta, Mr. Milind Palsule, Mr. Dinesh Lodha, Mr. Yasunobu Nishiyama and Mr. Haruto Iwata.

I would also like to thank my Customers Dr. Harsh Mahajan, Dr. Purshottam Lal, Dr. Bharat Aggarwal, Dr. Ravin Sharma, Dr. TS Dhillon, Dr. Yudhvir Gupta, Dr. GC Gupta, Dr.Dinesh Arora, Dr. Atul Krishna, Dr. OP Gupta and Dr. VK Gupta, Dr. Sanjay Sharma, Dr. DS Yadav, Dr. TBS Buxi, Mr. Rahil Shah, Dr. Nilesh Shah, Dr. Shilpa Lad, Dr. Suma Chakraborthy, Dr. Sujit Kar Purkayastha, Dr. Emmanual, Dr. Uday Patil, Dr. Surendra Reddy, Dr. Suman, Mr. Sohjwal Vohra and many many more interacting with whom day in and day out, I learnt many valuable lessons.

Apart from these, I would also like to express my deepest gratitude to my teachers who shaped me from my primary school Sh. Umed Singh ji, Sh. Naphe Singh Ji, Sh Satbir Singh ji and opened my mind. They not only taught me History, Geography and Maths and Science, but also instilled a deep-rooted and everlasting (thirsty) love for knowledge. Thanks are also due to my teachers from IIM Lucknow (Noida campus) - Prof. Dr.Archana Shukla for teaching me Organization Structure and Prof. Dr. Anand for teaching Project Finance, Dr. SC Bansal Balance Sheet, Dr. Rajiv Kumra and Dr. Anita for teaching us Marketing Management.

In addition to these, I am extending my heart-felt thanks to my Friends Mr. Arun Kumar, Arnab Jana, Rajesh Kapoor, Prabal Ghosh, Jyoti Shitole and many others who helped me become a better person in life.

I would also like to give credit to the culture of the place where I lived - a small village Khanpur Gurukul Kalan Sonepat District Haryana. The Mantrochharan at Yagyashala, each morning as well as the stories of yogis, saints and Upanishads, have not only shaped my thinking, but have also guided and supported me during the myriad ups and downs of life.

I would also like to say big thank to Dr. Maua Maulick for providing all the support in making the book in this form. She has done this on request of my Wife Dr. Priti Nanda Sibal.

Last, but not least, my special thanks to my other influencers whose writings I read a lot like Viveknanda ji, Sudha Muthi Ji, Nandan Nilekani ji, Premji and Narayan Murty Ji and many other authors.

WHY THIS BOOK

As a successful salesperson, I have had the opportunity to meet numerous people who have impacted my thinking in various ways. One of them was young Anand, a morose middleorder executive. He was upset because he didn't get the promotion he was expecting. This is a very bad field, I wish I hadn't joined it, "He said." I tried to encourage and draw him to come out of his negative mindset, but he remained unconvinced.

It's easy for you to say everything will be all right Sir, , because life has been a cakewalk for you, "He said".

That got me thinking: I feel thankful for life has always been a cakewalk for me. Indeed,it is, for anyone who think in a particular way or do the things in a certain way.

It's not like I always wanted to work in Sales or that I flew to just landed on the top. I have had my share of ups and downs and I have tried to use each as a stepping-stone for better things.

I would like to share my experiences so that you can utilize them in your work and also become successful in Sales.

When I was studying, I never wanted to become a salesperson or come to sales. At that time, I was dreaming of going to R&D or NASA or develop new products, but as luck would have it, I joined Sales.

I slowly worked my way up while working with Wipro GE Healthcare and was doing very well for almost a decade. However, then one fine day, a younger person with no experience in the healthcare sector was made my boss, just because he had an MBA degree.

I found it very demotivating and demoralizing. But I couldn't help but admit to myself that I was outdated. I was not familiar with Portals Five Forces models or comfortable with many business terminologies. At the age of 40 I decided to reinvent myself and get back into the game.

I gave the entrance exam for admission at IIM Lucknow (Noida campus Part-Time MBA program). Although I failed at my first attempt, I cleared in the second attempt and there was no looking back after thart.

And that is perhaps the first lesson I would like to share – to persevere and never give up.

Chapter 1

WHAT IS SALES?

Sales is a very important part of any company,regardless of its size. No matter how good or brilliant a particular product or service might be, if it is not sold, it cannot make money. Money is important to do research, refine your product and expand your reach, hire more employees and improve upon your services.

Thomas Alva Edison, the great inventor, was also a great salesperson. He began by selling newspapers. He then went on to sell his ideas. He once said, "Anything that won't sell, I don't want to invent. Its sale is proof of utility, and utility is success."

My definition of sales is commitment to provide product or services profitably to the customers and successful sales is to go beyond your commitment, to add value to customer. In Sales, true contentment comes only if your customer says you delivered more than you promised.

I still treasure one such compliment from a doctor at the Holy Family hospital after we installed the Hi-Speed CT/e Dual in the year 2002. After completing Teleradiology he could now report from home during night-time emergency. I gained not only a loyal client but also a good friend. Subsequently, I sold 16 Slice CT and many other projects to this Hospital.

Here is another real—life incident. I was working with L&T at Jaipur as Customer Engineer. I was very energetic and restless person. I would finish the daily assignments in just a few hours and ask for new tasks.

We had some 18 installations of Ultrasound machines and my boss told me to write letter for AMC and CMC. I did all these just within two days. My boss asked me to follow and close the AMC and CMC contracts. I took all the contracts in 30 days and solved some of the toughest and long-pending issues in the next 30 days, which were lingering on for years together. Though the job was done, but I was again without any work. I asked my boss to assign me some more work. He told me to meet the Health Secretary of Rajasthan to explain about our products.

In the meanwhile, I got some news from my boss that I have been transferred to Chandigarh with immediate effect. I was very confused over my transfer order, as it was just within two and a half months of joining the job.

I asked my boss the reason why I am being transferred in less than 3 months of joining, but he did not tell me the reason. And I was not in a position to insist (he was my boss!).

Later, I came to know that there were zero sales in Chandigarh and the branch was in a mess. I was transferred there as a troubleshooter and Branch Head for Medical division with immediate effect.

I was taken aback by the huge responsibility, particularly as I had no experience in handling sales.

I was open about my doubts and communicated my shortcomings to my seniors and my apprehensions that it would take me quite some time to put things in order at the branch particularly since Punjab was just coming out of the dark period of terrorism.

I was lucky to have supportive seniors who sent me off with a pat on my back. Bolstered by their confidence in my abilities, I plunged headlong into the mammoth task that awaited me.

I was confident that with my hard work and dedication and single-minded attention, I would be able to achieve even difficult any task.

Within a week of joining, I was called to the Regional Office, Delhi for a meeting.

On the way, I stayed the night with my parents at Panipat. Over there, I dropped in to the small Nursing Home nearby for a courtesy visit. The owner was mulling about buying an ESU Electro-surgical Unit and Monitor. I leaped at the chance and promptly gave him the requisite quotation and he too instantly closed the order worth 100,000 rupees.

And that's how my first sale happened - easy as pie.

But only because I seized the day.

And followed up punctiliously. On the way back I carried the Monitor and ESU, delivered it, made sure it was installed and in proper working condition and collected the balance payment.

I never looked back after this and kept on meeting customer after customer and closing orders after order.

The secret of my success was cold calling, meeting customers and giving complete solutions to their problems. I was following a customer for ultrasound sales and customer was not getting convinced to buy as we did not have any installation in that city. Moreover, the competitors were giving negative feedback about us.

Due to patient load, meeting the client was difficult despite several visits. So, one day after a number of failed visits, I left him a card apologizing for not being able to meet him and also a card detailing the additional NEW Features of our machine.

And that convinced him and got me the deal. Mere act of documenting the unique features of the product and adding world NEW actually got me this deal. So see how the world NEW Features has an effect!

So, Always Explain features with New Vigour!

Chapter 2

LOOSE CONNECTIONS

On my first day as a service engineer at a company, I was sent to a Delhi hospital to attend to a complaint. I had never seen an ICU before with lots of Monitors, Anesthesia machines, Defibrillator, IV lines, Central Nursing Station, etc. I went inside with my tool kit and was informed by the Nurse that the Monitor was dead. Overcoming my dread of the morbid surroundings, I checked and found that the power cable wires were loose.

I reconnected and tightened the loose wires in the plug and the monitor started functioning immediately.

Just a simple case of loose connections.

In my estimate, nearly half of life's problems are due to loose connections and are very simple and easily managed. We have loose connections with our friends, our neighbors, our relatives and all that we have to do is be proactive about it and find it, tighten it and get it running again. And often it is just a smile, a hello or a phone call.

Loose connections are everywhere and is a recurrent theme in this book as well.

Chapter 3

DIG DEEPER

While working as a service engineer at another company, we received a serious complaint from a client. It was written in legal language which threatened us with dire consequences if the money for the faulty machine was not refunded immediately. Apparently, the machine had already been replaced twice without resolution of the problem.

I reached the city after an overnight journey from Jaipur, and went straight to meet the surgeon. He was busy and kept me waiting for almost 10hours.

When I finally got to meet him, he blasted me and demanded a full refund along with penalty. I requested him to let me check the machine. He refused saying, lots of engineers had come and tried something which make the machine work but after they leave the same problem reappeared. I requested again to let me have a look. He reluctantly agreed.

I checked the machine and tightened all connections and to our surprise, machine started working. The surgeon got annoyed and said, see this is what I was saying, now you will leave and it will stop working again.

"How do you use this machine?" I asked.

"I am the top most surgeon of the city and you are asking me how am I using this machine?" He snapped.

"Sorry Sir. No offence. I just wanted to understand the problem" , I said politely.

He told me that he was carrying this machine to nearby hospitals in a radius of about 100 km and doing surgeries there and in this way, using this machine as a mobile machine.

"How are you transporting this machine?", I asked.

He told me that he was using packing it a suitcase and showed it to me.

Then I asked him, "How do you keep it?" He replied, "Straight in vertical position."

And that was the root cause of the problem. Keeping it vertical in a vehicle for long periods of time interfered with its functioning. The horizontal position would be more compatible. As expected, the problem never re-occurred and when I visited customer 6 months later and he was extremely happy.

Take Away Point

Dig deeper and try to find the root cause and do not give ad hoc stop-gap solutions.

Notes:

Chapter 4

CONVINCE; CONVINCE AND CONVINCE

This story is very close to my heart. I was trying to sell a 64 slice CT Scanner to a customer in Delhi. It was a big project worth almost a million dollars. We finally got this order after a lot of hard work which included demonstration at Chennai and numerous discussions on the physics and applications superiority of the machine. However, the competitors swung into action and they confused the customer with baseless adverse comments about the product such as very high heat dissipation, huge AC requirements, high dose, etc.

He was so shaken that even though the equipment had been shipped, he refused to take delivery of the machine and instead asked to cancel the order.

I swung into action and personally met the customer and narrated a story which I read in school. Perhaps you have also read it.

Once a priest went to perform a house-warming Pooja and the owner of House gave him a gift, a baby Goat. As the kid was too small to walk, he carried it on his shoulders.

There were three thieves who wanted the goat. Deciding to trick him, one of the thugs came and told the priest, "Why are you carrying a dog on your head?"

The priest was confused. He put the down to confirm that it was a goat.

He began walking again but had hardly gone 200 steps ahead, when another thug came and said to him, "Why are you carrying a cat on your head?" The priest was shaken and he checked once again. Convinced that it was a goat, he resumed his journey.

At a little distance ahead, the third thug came and asked him, "Why are you carrying a monkey on your head?" Now, the priest was thoroughly confused and lost faith in himself. He thought three people cannot be wrong. I must be wrong. He gave up the goat and went away while the thugs celebrated.

The customer was smart. He immediately caught what I was trying to say. He clapped me on my shoulder and said, "You are right! They were trying to mislead me and would have succeeded but for your perseverance. Send the consignment."

The takehome message here is never to take a deal or customer for granted. Any moment, anything can tilt the balance against you. The trick is to stay with the deal and on top of the game.

Chapter 5

NEVER SAY DIE

Once we were involved in a bidding war with a competitor at a new hospital that was installing a lot of new medical equipment and as fate would have it, we lost the deal.

Cut to four years later when the same hospital, wanted to upgrade their equipment and purchase and new products as well. Once again we were pitted against each other. But this time we won, even though it took us more than 2 years to close.

It was a very difficult and frustrating time for all of us, including the CEO who also held meetings with the customer. He was ready to give up and even told me to drop the deal as he believed it to be a dead end.

"Why are you wasting your time? Don't you have any other deal to follow?"

I was also very much disheartened as the quarter after quarter, I was not getting this deal. I visited this customer at least 50 times in a period of 2 years. I went to the CEO and I said politely, "Sir, I am coming and meeting you for the last 2 years and we have done every permutation and combination which you wanted. There were different payment plans as per your requirement. Whatever was required we provided. I just hope that you are not using me to cut a deal with our competitors."

The CEO was very much annoyed and even complained to my boss. I apologized and smoothed his ruffled feathers for the same.

Soon after that, the deal came through and we closed the order. This customer became our regular customer for years and today he is a great friend.

Moral of the Story

Work hard. Never give up and equally importantly, do not lose your patience. It could have easily gone wrong but luckily for me, the customer was a genuine person and I was not too proud to say sorry and let my hard work go down the drain. This can also be seen as Gita ka Gyan where I was not thinking of any result whether I would win or loose, I was playing my role as a Sale Person and was not getting disheartened with any remark and situation finally won this just because of this principle of Gita.

Chapter 6

NEVER LOSE YOUR HEART

This was a big client named Tac Group. We were trying to introduce our PACS Systems for complete 12 Hospital across country. We demonstrated our product during demonstration. Our application team did some mistake and we could not show images as our hard disk was not having the images which customers wanted to see and the customer was very adamant to not give us another chance and we were out of the deal.

But HOD of the Hospital left and new HOD joined and he started to see the products with new vigor and called us for meeting . Again we were in the game , we were able to demonstrate our product with flying colors and now we have made very innovative solution of pay per use Model after lot of brainstorming as per their requirements. After lots of negotiation on price, we got LOI (Letter of Intent) but this was one sided and there were many penalty

Clauses which were one-sided only, such as even if the Internet of Hospital is not working, this would be the responsibility of the company. These terms were not at all acceptable as there was no control over these things.

I was thinking it would be closed after some negotiations. We got into serious discussions, but the CIO of the hospital left from our side also our I.T. and Service head left. It got prolonged. Tac Group of Hospitals, got new CIO and he wanted to reverse the decision taken by his predecessor. We thought that as we negotiated prices and everything is closed now so we were very much convinced that we would be granted the order, but we lost this deal to the competitor as the competition reduced further 10% rates as compared to our prices. We lost the order but I never lost hope. We accepted their decision gracefully and moved ahead. After Six months, customers wanted to decide regarding the consumables business and this time we negotiated and got the complete project and to our surprise, this time we won a much bigger and better in terms of revenue and margin. Morale of the Story is that even if you lose a deal, don't lose the heart as this would not be the last deal from customer. Be persistent and remain positive.

This customer has taken lots of new products like FFDM Full Field Digital Mammography and Mobile DR products later on and our relationship is going great. Morale of the story is that we have to keep on working and sometimes we would lose and sometimes we would win but, we should not get disheartened and take the loss with stride and move on to another deal or try to make ourselves more competitive for the next deal.

Chapter 7

BE POSITIVE

There was a potential customer in Amritsar who was using our competitor's machine for the last 6 years and was happy with the image quality of the machine.

We attempted to convince him about the superiority of our product and explained him in detail the advantages like 1Sec Scan time, 3D Reconstruction, Colored 3D Rendering, SSD Surface Shaded 3D and MIP Maximum Intensity Projection and Minimum Intensity Projection software. In addition, there were other features and benefits of our machine like better mA, KV and Tube Capacity like 2MHU Tube with 200 mA output etc. The customer was slowly but surely being convinced about our product. Luckily for us, the competitor was complacent. They thought that this customer could not go anywhere as there was nobody who could sell off their existing machine.

Little did they know that we had a deal with the customer to first sell off his machine before we can get the order for new machine. I made a deal with a local radiologist to buy the older machine, but the client was apprehensive about selling his machine within 100 km radius as it would cut into his share of business. I went back to the market and after a lot of effort found another potential buyer, this time in Delhi.

After we sold the new machine, he became our regular customer and we got several orders for other high grade medical equipments as well.

This is an example of how to play the market, and try even if a competitor is in the lead. Never lose your cool with a customer, even if he changes the rules in the middle. Remember, the customer is always right and a satisfied customer is what brings you more business.

Chapter 8

INTEGRITY IS THE BEST POLICY

At a Medical College and Hospital in UP was looking to buy several machines such as CT Scanner, BMD, Mammography machine etc. When we went to meet the head of the department of radiology, he was very direct and blunt.

"What is in it for me?" He asked.

Knowing very well what he was referring to I chose to misunderstand him. I said we could give you everything you want—good machine, good service and good Application training.

But the radiologist was persistent. "What is in it for me?", He asked again.

I was in a fix as we never used to indulge in this sort of underhand dealings. I shook my head helplessly. Needless to say, the radiologist rejected us. But I didn't give up and bypassed him to contact the owner directly. He was a straightforward no-nonsense person and strictly warned us against any 'cut' system. We were only too happy to oblige him and gain a life-long loyal customer in the process, regardless of which company I was associated with.

Unbelievable though it may sound, after a gap of 5 years they finalized a 4 crore (0.70 Million USD approx) deal with us within a span of thirty minutes.

Despite the moral turpitude of our times, honesty and integrity are still valued. And once again the theory of long-term relationships is upheld. Always remember that the first order can be sold by any salesperson, but repeat orders comes because of service and personal relationships with customers.

I can quote several examples where customers opted for us because we were completely honest and our integrity was above board. Earlier, I had the impression that all people in the Government were corrupt and would never pass a deal without the mandatory cut. But over the years and after selling many machines, I have been lucky enough to meet doctors who appreciated and supported work ethics and timely service and application support more than any personal gains.

After working closely with the end-users for many years, I can proudly say that understanding their needs and providing solution with utmost integrity and honesty is the best way to win the deals.

Chapter 9

TOUGH COMPETITION? INNOVATE

This story is about a very renowned chain of Diagnostic Centres in India. This successful chain primarily used our competitor's equipment. However, we tried to enter their space by positioning our superior product best suited for their requirements. However, despite being impressed with our product after a lot of deliberations, they went with the competitor's product. Why? Because of their long-term relationship.

Although we were disheartened, we continued to negotiate and position our equipment for we knew they required two machines. And after a lot of negotiations, we cracked the deal.

To stay in the game and be more visible, we began organizing training workshops, CMEs (Continuing Medical Education) and public awareness programs where we invited leading doctors and opinion-makers to speak on the topic of the day. We also roped in doctors to write books and slowly more and more publications started coming out.

This not only increased our interaction with key personalities and opinion makers in the healthcare sector, but also helped build new relationships and win deals.

So, finally we not only cracked the deal, but also made this customer our key luminary and Radiologist here wrote the first book on Tomosynthesis and this Centre became our training centre and show site and this customer started giving training on breast imaging across the world.

Chapter 10

BE EARLY AND CONSULTATIVE SELLING CAN BE OF BIG HELP

It is a good strategy to identify a potential customer and be involved with them right from the planning stage. We met a doctor during a product launch who had come from abroad and was looking to build a hospital in India. We became associated with him at that stage itself when there was nothing except an idea and a dream. We brainstormed with them, gave our inputs on optimum utilization of equipment as per our knowledge of the requirements in the healthcare sector in the country. We helped them strategize and optimize their requirements so that they could choose the basic machines first and go for a bigger better machines later, once the hospital was better established. Like in this Hospital told him to go for Dual Slice CT instead of 16/64 Slice CT and Start with Entry level 1.5T MRI instead of 3T.

Once the hospital was set up, other companies joined the bandwagon but by then we had had a head start. We had formed a personal working relationship built on mutual respect and trust. And of course, we got the deal for keeping the customer's requirements first and not being in a hurry to sell without a care for their financial concerns.

While enlisting a new customer it is imperative that we keep our eye on the larger perspective and have a long-term goal rather than just that fiscal year's balance sheet. My association with this company is now over 15 years and we had bagged many projects as they continued to grow and require new machines and upgrades.

We were similarly associated with another big hospital that was set up in Delhi. We were closely involved in the conceptualization, design along with product requirements. We helped them understand global set ups and functioning. We even helped them shortlist young dynamic doctors for their hospital. We were on the verge of closing down our gas pipeline division but at their insistence, we undertook that project also. There came a time when their budget was exhausted and they opted to outsource the Radiology equipment. We played a major role in brokering this partnership. We got the order from a Radiology chain, but due to certain reasons, the Fire Completion certificate was delayed and Hospital project got delayed by over a year.

Frustration and misunderstandings cropped between the Hospital and Radiology service Provider who suffered huge monetary losses. Somehow, we pacified both parties and got them to some agreement.

In this way, we became not only a Sales company, but also a trusted partner and ally.

Always remember to work today with an eye to the future. Go beyond the call of duty and never say this is not my job. This is my mantra for life which helped me to grow and help others grow as well.

Notes:

Chapter 11

LEARN TO LISTEN

Once we got a legal notice from one of our customers for non-installation and not supplying the proper product to him.

The customer was of course very annoyed and took out his anger by keeping me waiting for almost the entire day. And then he blasted me. But I did not lose my temper. I kept my cool and tried to see things from his perspective.

A dealer had sold him the machine and had not bothered to even install it properly. I apologized and offered to not only rectify the problem but also offered to give a coveted instrument at a vastly discounted price. Needless to say, the customer was satisfied and he not only withdrew his case but also placed an order for another high-end machine. He too went beyond the limits of a business relationship and was of immense help when my father met with an accident for which I am deeply indebted.

My only submission through this incident is that sometimes giving a patient listening ear to customer grievances is enough to melt the toughest of customers.

The Morale of the Story

Be a part of the solution not the problem.

Chapter 12

HUMOR SELLS

Once I was waiting to meet one of the top Cardiologists of Delhi at his Hospital. He was a very busy doctor and often made us wait for long periods sometimes, fruitlessly.

This time I was successful but when I told him I wanted to give him a 15-minute presentation on the key features of the latest software, he said, "Mr. Sibal, I don't give this much time even to my wife."

I closed my laptop and stood up holding out my hand, "Sorry Sir, if your wife also cannot get this much time, then even 1 minute time that you gave me is enough."

He burst out laughing.

After this incident, I not only got the deal but also became good friends. He went out of his way to give his time and medical expertise when my father had a heart attack for which I will be eternally grateful.

Morale of the story is never lose your temper with a customer and always try to lighten up a stressful situation with a smile or a light-hearted comment.

Chapter 13

THINK BIG, THINK LONG–TERM

One More Story comes to my mind and this time the Customer was Dr. Mukhi and he was having a Diagnostic Centre and he was using a competitor's machine.

Once I tried to gain a customer who was already working with a competitor. We gave presentations and demonstrations which impressed the customer. The deal was all but signed. But then no deal is done until it is signed on the dotted line (and sometimes not even then!). Anyway the customer came back after a few days and said that even though we had handled the deal very well, they were going with the competitor's product. He shook my hand in apology and appreciation of my efforts. Swallowing my disappointment, I smiled back at him. "Never mind Sir. Next time."

"Next time." He nodded.

A couple of months later, the same customer called me to tip me off about a potentially huge deal with another client who was a friend of his.

He also told me that in case I went myself, the deal could be closed within a day. I wasted no time in contacting the customer and to my gratification, I could close an over one crore deal in one sitting. Sometimes one has to usually labor over for months, sometimes even for years. Maintaining good relationships with 'failed' customers also helps! You never know when they might need a new deal, an upgrade or give a positive reference.

Learn from your mistakes

Being in Sales, we always have to be bright and motivated. We have to make sure that we present a positive picture, not only to our customers but also our bosses. And in the process we often forget (deliberately) our losses.

But I am a firm believer of the great inventor and businessman Thomas Alva Edison who exhorted, "Never get discouraged if you fail. Learn from it. Keep trying."

No matter how painful and disturbing it may have been, after every loss I used to analyze the loss deeply.

Why I lost the deal? What could I have done differently and what should I not have done etc. our losses or failures teach us more than our successes.

As after loss, we make analysis and retrospect and after winning, we are on such a high that we don't even care to introspect.

For instance, when I lost an order upon looking back, I could see that I had missed certain basics of Sales. I had failed to do a background check on the customer requirements vis-a-vis available competition in the market — *i.e.* what were they offering in comparison to my offer.

For any sales cycle these are the points which I used to take care of

1. Proper product presentation
2. Understanding the requirement
3. Making right configuration
4. Demonstration of Machine with Features and Benefits
5. Competition product analysis & Customers Competition information and market analysis for customer
6. USPs of product
7. Proper comparison
8. Objection Handling
9. Negotiation cycle
10. Closing the Deal
11. After Closure, Launch of Product

I could look back and see wherever I have taken care of these points, I got success in more than 70% of cases with of price difference of about 5-10%.

Also, regarding pricing it is my experience that it is not the price alone but the value of the product and that you add to it in attitude. The customer must be convinced that you are there not just for the deal or the check but for the relationship. That you can be relied upon for any after sales service. Once the customer is satisfied, you can be sure that many deals will follow, sooner or later.

Chapter 14

MAKING ORGANISATION STRUCTURE THAT FOSTERS TEAM WORK & ENTREPRENEURIAL SKILLS

In any organization development of Organization Structure is the most important part. I learnt it from our teacher Prof. Archana Shukla. In my present organization, structure is based upon fundamental question which is the buying behavior of Customer.

So, Segmentation of Customers like Private– though Channel Network Govt.– Direct from Govt. Team

Corporate Customers–Direct Focus on Top 50 to 100 Corporates

This kind of Segmentation helps as buying behavior of customer is completely different in each segment. We could achieve almost 70-80% of market share due to direct quoting as we were quoting best rates without any hedging and we were in touch with customers at an early stage and working from scratch. As Govt. buys in bulk, their purchase price is the lowest and they provide the rate contracts for 2 years and once we get Rate Contracts, our Revenue increases and we keep on getting regular big business.

TI Concept: We hired 10 young MBA students from Amity University and stationed them in Tier2 and Tier 3 cities across country. Fostering Team work was very important. We have put Territory In charge – TI in Tier-2 and Tier-3 cities and their job was to support dealers in closing orders and providing technical support whenever needed. Their work was to support dealers and train Channel Partners Men Power and go with them for closing. This made a huge change and our winning ratio increased as these young team was very enthusiastic and worked very closely with Dealers. This increased our market share to almost 50% in this segment. The One Point I want to highlight is that the reason for success was team work and train Channel partners staff and help in closing their orders.

Corporate Customers

As we all know corporate customers work in different ways and their main point is in marketing support, Educational Tie-ups and getting the latest technology with new features and making awareness across the patient segment.

We fostered tie-ups with top corporates for providing trainings to young Doctors, technicians and these steps helped us to become their vendor of choice. We never wanted to become a push player. We started these programs so that Customers started asking, “Can we start these programs with them also?” So, we became their choice number one by helping them in accomplishing their goals.

Keeping Teams motivated is most important as I have seen motivated team player taking the Area or the State to different levels with his passion and enthusiasm. So, we designed incentive schemes which would make them entrepreneurs and they would try to increase the business.

Also, the most important point was interdependence like one team member was dependent on other to get the work done which fostered better bonding in Product/Modality/Regional Sales Team. This gave team the confidence to win and finally when team wins, it is used to give them huge motivation to other teams to win.

Every year we used to give awards for Best Teams and I would like to tell you that All Regions and Almost all the Modalities won awards in one or the other year means the trophy for best region kept on rotating. When I joined, South was the best Region and the next year West became better Region than East Region and the next year South and North combined won the trophy so there was all-around comprehensive growth across the regions.

So, it is important to have a healthy and winning environment in all Regions rather than focusing on only one Region.

I started two new concepts—the first one was CI concept which was Circle in-charge. In this we made circles and hired 20 Diploma Holders across the country, trained them for six months in Service, Application and Sales and then depending on their capability and company requirement, we put them their respective fields and these young guys ranging from age 18 years to 22 years, did wonderful job as young people have so much of energy and enthusiasm that once they start working they can work 24x7 and 365 days. Here, advice from Professor S.C. Bansal helped me. He told me once always hire from lower income groups and that would help them to get inclusion into middle class and they would do wonder with their hard work. The same thing happened. These young team members worked so hard that has given us lots of new information and ideas which were otherwise would not have been available to us. We started another program to higher young Application team from colleges directly and we hired from St. Stephens Hospital, Delhi and trained them and within a 2 month of time, they started giving us great results. So, taking young team members from campus worked wonderfully well with us and we could create a great balance between the young and old team.

Basics of doing the numbers or completing your target is only one that we have to increase our customer base, need to add more customers to our Lead base, like sometimes people say that this event did not do well or we could not get the crowd from this event. I say otherwise there is always customer around. You need to attract them to your stall and you need to understand customers deeply. Also, I always motivate team members and keep awards for Team who brings maximum customer to booth and also motivate them and prepare them to do that. Giving awards for most knowledgeable customers is also a great strategy.

Only one strategy works in the end which creates motivation in

Employees, Customers and all the stakeholders.

These are the basics of achieving any target.

Chapter 15

WINNING CYCLE

Multiply your Leads by Meeting more Customers – at least 2 New Customers/day

This Would give rise to Strong Prospect Base

This would Lead to Order Pond

And from Order Pond Strong Long Term Relationship would

Multiply your Leads

Diagram for the same.

WINNING CYCLE

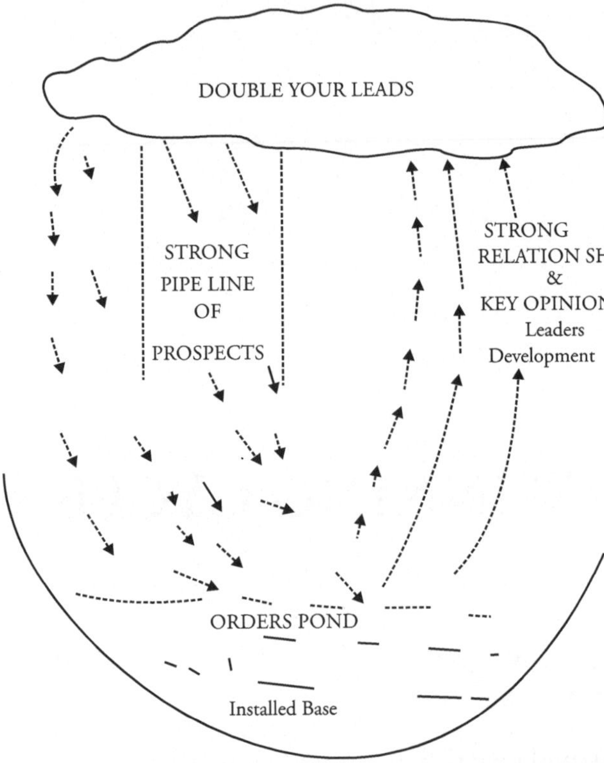

SUSTAINABLE CUSTOMER ACQUISITIONS

I would like that salespeople who read this book can share their experiences and I would like to make them part of this book during the next revisions of this book. You can share your stories at shekhar.sibal@gmail.com with subject my experiences with sales so that one can learn from each other.

Best Regards

–Chander Shekhar Sibal